HOW TO SE
in a
JUNGLE

Written by
Anita Ganeri
Illustrated by
Rob Shone

SIMON & SCHUSTER
YOUNG BOOKS

About the author: **Anita Ganeri** has written and edited over 50 books for children, mainly on natural history and the natural world. She has travelled widely and has just returned from a trip to the jungles of Madagascar.
About the consultant: **Antony Mason** is a travel writer and author of books for children on geography and exploration. In the course of his travels, he has visited jungles in South-east Asia, South America and the Caribbean.
About the survival expert: **John Fisher** has served with the British Army Special Forces for 25 years and is trained in survival techniques for jungle and desert terrains. He has personal experience of surviving in the jungles of Malaysia.

Copyright © S•W Books 1993

Designed and conceived by
S•W Books
28 Percy Street
London W1P 9FF

First published in Great Britain in 1993 by
Simon & Schuster Young Books
Campus 400
Maylands Avenue
Hemel Hempstead
Herts HP2 7EZ

All rights reserved

This book is sold subject to the condition that it shall not, by way of trade or otherwise, be lent, re-sold, hired out, or otherwise circulated without the publisher's prior consent in any form of binding or cover other than that in which it is published and without a similar condition including this condition being imposed on the subsequent purchaser.

Printed and bound in Belgium by
PROOST International Book Production

British Library Cataloguing in Publication Data available

ISBN 0 7500 1367 2
ISBN 0 7500 1368 0 (pb)

CONTENTS
WHERE ON EARTH?
4
WHERE IN THE WORLD?
6
SHELTERING FROM THE ENVIRONMENT
8
EATING WITHOUT BEING EATEN
12
GETTING ON WITH THE LOCALS
22
GETTING ABOUT AND OUT
28
RAINFOREST SURVIVAL
30
GLOSSARY
31
INDEX
32

INTRODUCTION

If you suddenly found yourself in the middle of the jungle, how do you think you'd cope? Would you know how to fend off mosquitoes, rig up a shelter or spear a fish? What if you came face to face with a jaguar or disturbed a sleeping snake? Don't worry - help is at hand! Tribal people have lived in the world's jungles for thousands of years, relying on their special survival skills. They'll be able to teach you a thing or two. All you need to do is read on and discover more about the jungle world and the people, plants and animals that live in it. There are survival tips and stories of intrepid jungle explorers to spur you on your way...

WARNING! DON'T TRY ANY OF THE SURVIVAL TIPS IN THIS BOOK, EXCEPT UNDER THE STRICT SUPERVISION OF A JUNGLE TRIBESMAN.

WHERE ON EARTH?

The word 'jungle' comes from an ancient Indian word which means a thick tangle of trees and plants. What we usually mean by jungles are the tropical rainforests which grow along the Equator, in places where it is hot, wet and steamy all year round. The patch of rainforest below shows you what to expect inside the jungle. Can you see how the trees form layers?

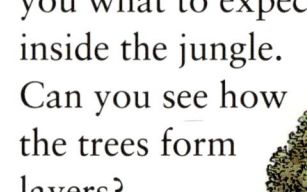

WHAT IS A JUNGLE?

From a river bank or the edge of a clearing, a jungle lives up to its reputation as a misty, eerie mass of trees and creepers. Here the trees crowd together, to make the most of the light. It's different inside the jungle - surprisingly clear and easy to walk through, although it may be rather gloomy. There are strange noises - birds cackling, monkeys squawking and the drip, drip, drip of the rain. But many of the noisiest jungle animals only come out at night, so the volume isn't very loud. There's a strong smell from the wet leaves which are decaying on the forest floor.

Canopy
The leaves and branches of the canopy trees form a thick, green roof over the rainforest. They get the most sun and rain.

Understorey
The understorey is made up of smaller trees, such as palms, and saplings struggling to reach the light.

Shrub layer
Small, woody shrubs, herbs, ferns and the smallest trees form the lowest layer.

AMAZON RAINFOREST

Emergent layer
A few, very tall trees poke up above the rest of the rainforest. These are the emergents, growing to the dizzy heights of 60m.

JUNGLE SPOTTING
Millions of plants and animals live in the jungles. Use them to identify which jungle you're in. There are toucans and jaguars in South America; tarsiers and rafflesia flowers in South-east Asia. If you spot a mountain gorilla, you're in Africa.

TYPES OF RAINFOREST
There are different kinds of rainforest. Cloud forests grow high on mountain slopes. Montane forests are found lower down. This book is mostly about lowland forests.

Cloud forest
Montane forest
Lowland forest
Flooded forest
Flood plain
River

Forest floor
Very little sunlight reaches the forest floor, so it is always gloomy and thick with fallen and decaying leaves.

WHERE IN THE WORLD?

Rainforests grow along the Equator, in the areas known as the tropics. The biggest forests are in Central and South America, central Africa and South-east Asia. There are also small patches in India, China, Australia, Madagascar, Papua New Guinea and on some of the islands in the Caribbean. Rainforests cover about six per cent of the Earth. They were once twice the size they are today, and they're still disappearing fast.

JUNGLES OF THE WORLD

Over 70 countries in the world can claim to have some jungle, although it may be only the tiniest patch. The largest jungle of them all is the Amazon rainforest in South America. It grows along the banks of the mighty River Amazon and its many tributaries, mostly in Brazil, and is bigger than all the other jungles put together. It was once very, very much bigger than it is today. The rainforests are being cut down and destroyed at an alarming rate. To clear space for farming and ranching, sixty soccer pitches worth of forest are being cut down every minute...

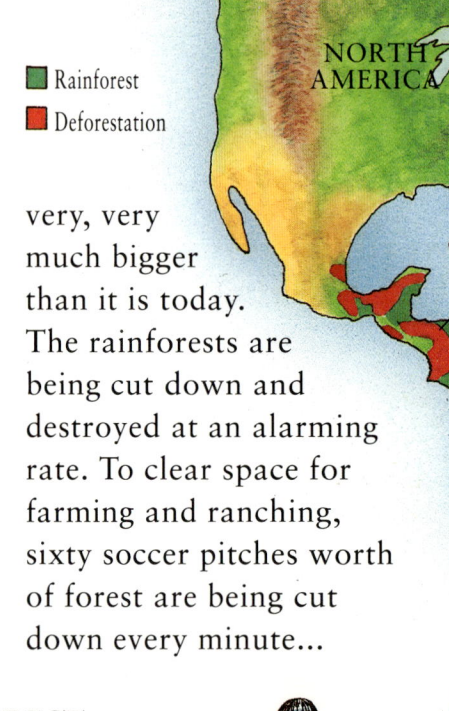

The Amazon rainforest is twice the size of India.

PEOPLE OF THE RAINFOREST

There are thought to be about 1.5 million tribespeople living in the rainforests. They have survived there for thousands of years, getting everything they need from the forest around them. They hunt forest animals, and gather fruit, roots and nuts for food and medicines. Some are settled and live in one place. Others are nomads, moving around in search of food. They know the jungle better than anyone.

1
Yanomami
Amazonia

2
Wai Wai
Guyana

3
Camayura
Mato Grosso,
Brazil

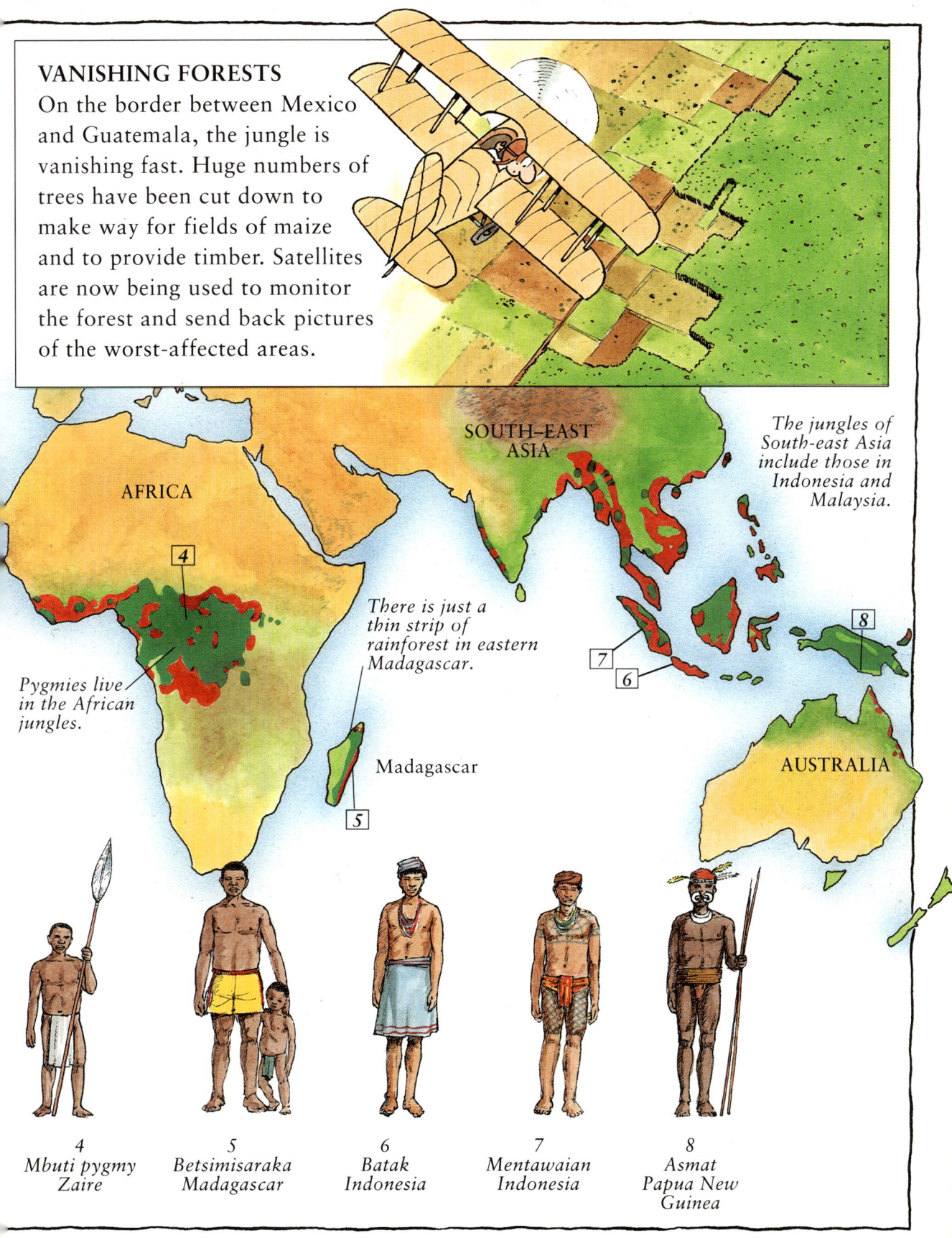

VANISHING FORESTS

On the border between Mexico and Guatemala, the jungle is vanishing fast. Huge numbers of trees have been cut down to make way for fields of maize and to provide timber. Satellites are now being used to monitor the forest and send back pictures of the worst-affected areas.

The jungles of South-east Asia include those in Indonesia and Malaysia.

There is just a thin strip of rainforest in eastern Madagascar.

Pygmies live in the African jungles.

SOUTH–EAST ASIA

AFRICA

Madagascar

AUSTRALIA

4 Mbuti pygmy Zaire

5 Betsimisaraka Madagascar

6 Batak Indonesia

7 Mentawaian Indonesia

8 Asmat Papua New Guinea

SHELTERING FROM THE ENVIRONMENT

Now that you know a bit about the jungle and have met some of its inhabitants, let's get down to the business of survival. In the jungle, as everywhere else, the weather has a great effect on how people live, what they wear, what they eat and the dangers they face. Rainforest tribespeople have adapted to the conditions but you may find they take some getting used to.

WEATHER AND CLIMATE

The jungle is hot and wet all year round. The temperature ranges from 20°C at night to 30°C during the day. Up to 25cm of rain can fall each day, often in afternoon thunderstorms. The air is very sticky because of the high humidity. There are no real seasons in the jungle - just hot and wet, and hotter and wetter. The chart shows the average temperature and rainfall of three places including the Amazon rainforest.

	Average total rainfall Jan / July	Maximum average temp °C Jan / July
London	54 mm / 57 mm	6 / 22
New York	94 mm / 107 mm	3 / 28
Amazon Basin	249 mm / 58 mm	31 / 32

(Temp = °Celsius)

Hair keeps heat in and protects against the cold, so rainforest people have very little hair on their bodies.

Rainforest people have small, compact builds. This allows them to lose more heat from their bodies and to keep cool.

In the jungle, people don't wear much - there's no point. Some wear just a loincloth and some jewellery or make-up.

Rainforest people don't sweat very much. Sweat usually cools the body, but not in the humid air of the jungle.

Broad feet help people to climb trees to reach fruit and honey, and to stop them sinking into the muddy jungle floor.

ADAPTING TO THE CLIMATE

Rainforest people have physical features which help them to survive in the heat of the jungle. But you may find it a very hot, sticky place to start with. If you sweat a lot - and you probably will - you'll lose not only water but salt, too. Dissolve some salt or a salt tablet in water and drink this to restore the balance. Otherwise you'll soon feel dizzy, sick and tired. Try to stay cool - the salt in sweat also attracts mosquitoes!

Bush hat

Torch

You, on the other hand, should cover up well. Long sleeves and trousers will stop you getting bitten, scratched or sunburnt.

A water-proof bag is useful for keeping any spare clothes, matches and food dry.

Good boots are a must for trekking through the jungle. Wrap bark or cloth around your ankles as protection against insects and snakes.

EXPLORER FACTS

An American explorer, Eric Hansen, spent many months in the jungles of Borneo. He travelled on foot and in a dug-out canoe and ate whatever he found - monkeys, deer, lizards, boa constrictors, wild pigs and fruit.

SURVIVAL TIP 1

Leeches live on blood! They won't hurt you but never pull them off. The wound may get infected. Dab them with salt or let them fall off naturally when they're full.

UNDER COVER

The type of home or shelter that a rainforest tribe has depends on its particular way of life. Nomadic tribespeople wander about from place to place in search of food. Their shelters are only temporary and quite makeshift. Some people build semi-permanent huts which last for two or three years. Others live more settled lives. All the materials needed to build a home are collected from the forest - wood, bamboo poles, palm leaves and vines.

SURVIVAL TIP 2

Build your own shelter away from the river, in case it floods in the night. Make two A–shapes out of branches. Join them together with two long poles. Lay shorter branches over these. Cover the whole thing with your mosquito net.

This type of house is called a maloca. It is home to up to 30 members of a South American tribe, called the Barasana.

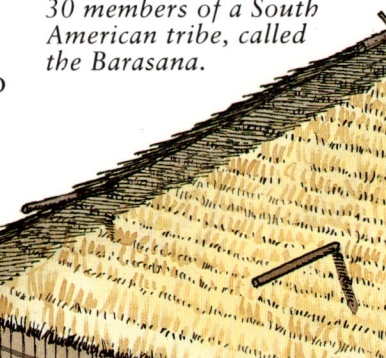

The maloca is a frame of wooden poles, tied together with vines and covered in palm leaves.

The front, or east, door is used by the men and by guests.

Maloca

SURVIVAL TIP 3

Centipedes, scorpions and snakes like nothing better than warm places to sleep in. Give your clothes and boots a good shake before putting them on, to get rid of unwelcome visitors.

EATING WITHOUT BEING EATEN

The jungle is full of things to eat, but you have to know where to look and what to avoid. Rainforest people live mainly by hunting animals and gathering fruit, roots and nuts. They also go fishing, and some tribes farm small plots of land in the middle of the jungle. Over hundreds of years, they have built up a huge store of knowledge about which animals and plants are good, or safe, to eat.

HUNTERS AND WEAPONS

In rainforest tribes, it is the men who go off hunting. They know exactly how to find animals by following their tracks and scent. They stalk their prey silently through the jungle undergrowth, then use blow–pipes, bows and arrows, spears or nets to bring it down or trap it.

Arrow-poison frog

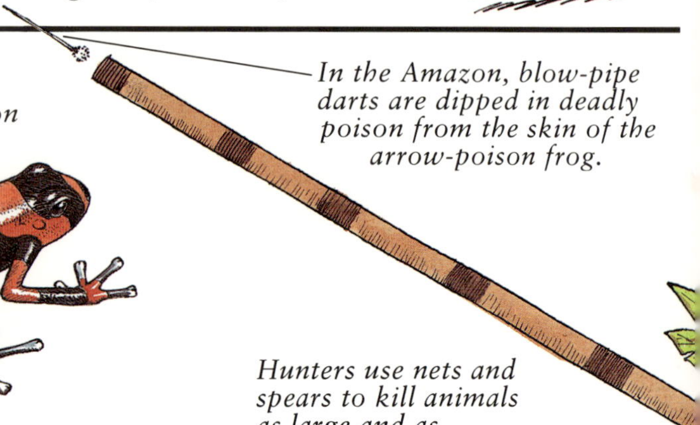

In the Amazon, blow-pipe darts are dipped in deadly poison from the skin of the arrow-poison frog.

Hunters use nets and spears to kill animals as large and as dangerous as forest elephants.

Pygmies hunt with bows and arrows, dipped in plant poisons or hardened in the fire. They hardly ever miss.

Apart from traditional weapons, some people also have shotguns. But the noise of gunfire often scares the animals away and many people prefer their silent arrows and darts for hunting.

ANIMALS FOR FOOD

Many rainforest animals are hunted for food. They include wild pigs, peccaries and antelope, together with more exotic creatures such as monkeys, toucans, tapirs, tree snakes and armadillos. A Yanomami hunter from the Amazon rainforest will not eat any animal he catches himself. He swaps his catch with another hunter in the tribe.

Woolly monkey
Tree snake
Forest elephant
Toucan
Anteater
Capybara
Tapir
Wild pig
Peccary
Armadillo

Amazon hunters use blow-pipes nearly two metres long to shoot poisoned darts at monkeys, birds and other prey.

EXPLORER FACTS

In 1541, Francisco de Orellana became the first European to travel the length of the Amazon River. On the way, he was attacked by warriors who looked like the women Amazon warriors of Greek mythology.

MAKING A BLOW-PIPE

A blow-pipe is made from a hollow reed or stem of bamboo fitted inside a hard, wooden outer casing. A wooden mouthpiece is cut to shape and added at one end. With his blow-pipe, a hunter can hit a target 30m away.

Inner tube
Outer casing
Finished blow-pipe
Wooden mouthpiece

GOOD FOOD GATHERING

Every day, the women and children gather fresh food from the forest. They collect fruit, nuts and berries and dig up roots and tubers, using sticks sharpened to a point. Grubs, beetles and other insects are added for extra protein. They are found inside rotten tree trunks, under logs and scuttling about under the tree bark. Special trips are made to collect honey from the nests of wild bees. Pygmies in Africa are guided to the bees' nests by the honeyguide bird.

Manioc plant

Beer is made from manioc bread, fermented in boiled manioc juice.

Manioc beer

Valuable honey is traded for other goods or used to sweeten food.

Maize

Yam

Salt

Manioc tuber

Manioc bread

Sweet pepper

Okra

Drink of boiled manioc juice

1. Manioc is peeled and grated.
2. The juice is squeezed out.
3. The juice is boiled.
4. Bread is made from the pulp.

PREPARING MANIOC

The tubers of the manioc plant are a staple food in the Amazon. But manioc has to be carefully prepared to get rid of the poison it contains. The tubers are peeled and grated, then any poisonous juice is squeezed out and boiled to make it safe. The pulp is made into flour or bread.

14

SURVIVAL TIP 4

Ants are full of protein and make a nourishing snack. But you must always cook them for at least six minutes to get rid of the poisonous formic acid inside them.

UNUSUAL JUNGLE GRUB

There are some unusual delicacies on the jungle menu. Starters might be caterpillar paste soup or roast locusts, followed by iguana or snake steak, toucan with palm tips and manioc bread. And to finish, durian fruit (it's smelly, but tasty) and honey!

Mangos, bananas, guavas, papayas and pineapples grow wild in the jungle.

How do you fancy an iguana steak or some snake and anteater stew?

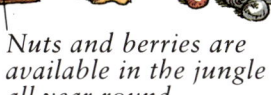

Nuts and berries are available in the jungle all year round.

Caterpillar paste soup

Grubs, beetles, locusts and other creepy crawlies are roasted or eaten raw. They are very good for you, believe it or not!

JUNGLE SHOPPING LIST
Chocolate
Coffee
Brazil nuts
Chewing gum
Chicken (descended from the Malaysian jungle fowl)
Sweet pepper
Ginger
Nutmeg
Black pepper
Avocados

Many of the things we eat come originally from the rainforests. Look out for them next time you go shopping.

EXPLORER FACTS

In 1893, Mary Kingsley set off from England to study the cannibal Fang tribe in Africa. She was spared from the pot herself but once shared a room with a bag of human bits.

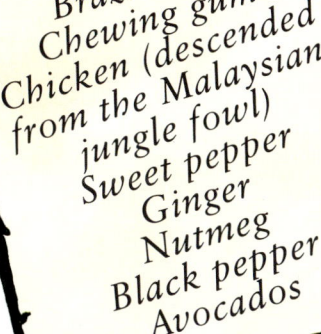

GONE FISHING

Many rainforest people rely on fish to provide protein in their diets. They fish from the shallow water by the river bank or from dug-out canoes (find out how to make a canoe on page 29). If they make a bumper catch, the extra fish is smoked and stored.

Various pieces of fishing tackle are used by jungle people. It includes nets, hooks and lines, traps, spears, bows and arrows and even machetes. Insects, berries and worms are used as bait.

Nets are made of vines and even from extra strong spiders' webs.

Using a bow and arrow for fishing needs great skill...and patience!

To make fish easier to catch, poisonous plant juice is sprinkled in the water. The stunned fish are scooped up in nets.

Hooks are made from thorns or bunches of thorns tied together.

SURVIVAL TIP 5

When you're spearing a fish, make allowances for the way the water makes the fish appear to be in a different place. Aim at the fish itself, not at the place where it seems to be.

The fish you see

Light bent by water

Aim here

The real fish

FOREST FARMING

Some rainforest people grow their own crops, in small plots or 'gardens'. They clear a patch of jungle and plant maize, bananas, sweet potatoes and, of course, manioc! Each family builds itself a house of vines, palm leaves and saplings, and tends its own garden. House and garden are abandoned after two or three years when the soil's goodness is used up. Left to its own devices, the jungle quickly grows back again.

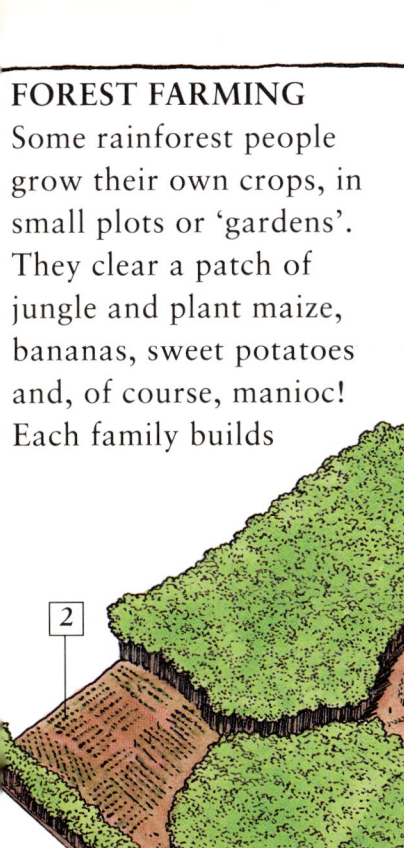

EXPLORER FACTS

The naturalist Henry Walter Bates (1825–1892), spent 11 years in the Amazon rainforest. He collected 15,000 specimens, mostly of insects. Over half had never been seen before.

Key
1. The forest is cleared and burned.
2. The garden is farmed.
3. Bananas still grow after the other crops are finished.
4. The jungle grows back over the abandoned garden.

THE FOREST GARDEN

To rainforest people, the whole jungle is like a huge garden. They grow their crops in it and can also harvest the jungle's own supply of fruit, nuts and berries.

BEWARE - DANGEROUS ANIMALS!

Although man-eating tigers are few and far between, they do exist! Beware, too, of the other dangerous animals in the jungle. They're not all as big as tigers or jaguars. The most deadly are the arrow-poison frogs. Rainforest people have had years of practice in knowing what to hunt and what to avoid. Your best bet is to treat all animals with respect - they are unlikely to attack you unless you tease or frighten them or their young. If you do come face to face with a tiger, however, FREEZE. Try to STAY CALM and back off or step to the side very, very slowly ...

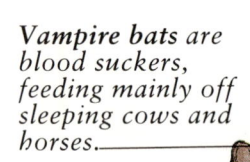

Vampire bats are blood suckers, feeding mainly off sleeping cows and horses.

Watch out for the sting in the tail of any *scorpions*.

SURVIVAL TIP 6

The smallest animal to fear is the mosquito. It spreads diseases which can be fatal, such as malaria. Keep well covered up, especially at dusk. Cover your head with a T-shirt or a hat and mosquito net. Use insect repellent!

Bird-eating spiders, or tarantulas, are large and hairy but have quite mild poison.

Jaguars and tigers are the top predators in the jungle.

One drop of the poison in the *arrow-poison frog's* skin is strong enough to kill a monkey.

FER DE LANCE

The fer de lance is deadly poisonous. The explorer, Sir Percy Fawcett, claimed that local people in South America placed these snakes in tubes and used them as lethal weapons.

JUNGLE PLANTS

The hot, steamy conditions in the rainforest are perfect for plants. They thrive in the year-round warmth and wetness. There are tall trees, bushy shrubs, vines strong enough to swing on, exquisite orchid flowers. There are plants which provide food, medicines and drugs, and raw materials. One of the main problems that plants face is the competition for light. Many have found ways round this - by climbing up other plants (vines) or growing high up on the branches of trees (epiphytes).

Rafflesia flower

THE JUNGLE INDOORS
Many of our house plants originally came from the jungle. They include rubber plants, parlour palms and bromeliads.

SURVIVAL TIP 7

Beware the deadly strychnine fruits. They look like oranges. The wait-a-while plant holds you tighter when you pull away.

Bromeliads grow high up on tree branches. Water collects in tiny pools formed by their leaves.

The *aroid* clings to tree trunks with its short roots. The aroid family includes Swiss cheese plants.

Local people chew *coca leaves*. The leaves are also made into the illegal drug, cocaine.

EXPLORER FACT

The first European to see wild rubber was a French explorer, La Condamine, in 1736. Until 1876, rubber was only grown in Brazil. Then a botanist, Sir Henry Wickham, smuggled some seeds out. Huge rubber plantations were later planted in Malaysia.

Orchids grow on tree branches. Their roots dangle in the air, taking in moisture.

Chocolate is made from the seeds of the **cocoa tree**. There are up to 70 seeds in each pod.

MEDICINAL PURPOSES

A quarter of all medicines come from the jungle. They include the rosy periwinkle from Madagascar. It is used to treat children with leukaemia (blood cancer). Local people use thousands of plants for medicinal purposes.

Rosy periwinkle

Strangler fig

STRANGLER FIGS

Strangler fig seeds are dropped on tree branches by birds or bats. As they grow, they send roots down to the ground to take up water and minerals. The roots surround and smother the tree.

SURVIVAL TIP 8

There is plenty of water in the jungle, but you need to make it safe to drink. Always boil it to get rid of germs or use water purifying tablets if you have some. Pitcher plants are a good source of water, but you would be well advised to filter it carefully to get rid of any creepy crawlies it contains.

GETTING ON WITH THE LOCALS

You know the saying, 'When in Rome, do as the Romans'? Well, the same applies to the rainforest. The local people have their own culture, customs, languages, beliefs... and taboos. They'll be quite happy to see you as long as you respect their way of life. After all, they've been around the rainforest much longer than you have. And don't worry - there aren't any cannibals or headhunters any more, or at least very few!

MYTHS

Most rainforest people worship the spirits of the forest which, they believe, live in the trees and animals. And they have plenty of stories and myths to explain the world they live in.

In a Brazilian myth, a deer marries a jaguar's daughter. The animals are in human form, so he doesn't realise what she is. He goes to visit her parents and is horrified that they have killed a deer to eat. In return, he brings back a dead jaguar from his hunting trip. The deer tells his in-laws that he keeps his eyes open while he's asleep. Thinking he's sleeping, they run away. He, of course, sees them and makes his own escape.

A myth from Papua New Guinea tells of an ogre who was half man, half pig. He ate all but two of his children. They

managed to kill him. His body was cut up and cooked so that everyone could eat a piece and share his great strength.

SURVIVAL TIP 9

Rainforest people speak many different languages. But they also have other ways of communicating. To send messages, Waorani hunters kick tree trunks which makes a booming sound.

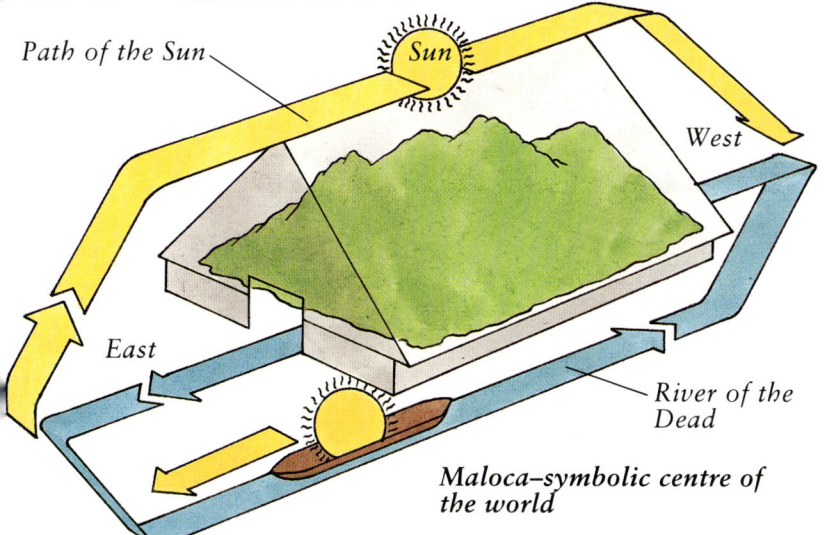

Maloca—symbolic centre of the world

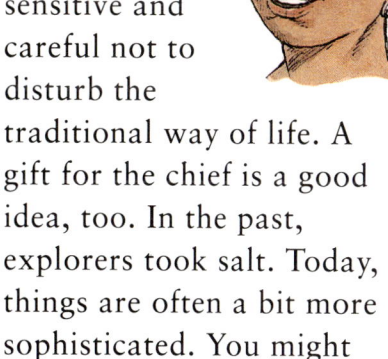

MEETING NEW FACES

If you don't know any of the local languages, a friendly smile will usually get you a warm welcome. Always show respect for the tribespeople you meet. Be sensitive and careful not to disturb the traditional way of life. A gift for the chief is a good idea, too. In the past, explorers took salt. Today, things are often a bit more sophisticated. You might see pots, pans and steel knives in the headman's hut.

THE MALOCA WORLD

The Barasana people of the Amazon rainforest see their maloca, or home, as a model of the world itself. The roof represents the sky, the support posts are the mountains and the horizontal roof pole is the path of the Sun across the sky. They imagine that the River of the Dead flows underneath the maloca from west to east. When the Sun sets at night in the west, it drops into the river and is carried along under the house to rise in the east next morning.

EXPLORER FACTS

The missionary and musician, Albert Schweizer (1875-1965), respected the customs of the African tribes he lived amongst. He won the Nobel Peace Prize for his work.

ARTS AND CRAFTS

Rainforest arts and crafts are linked very closely with a tribe's way of life, its beliefs and myths. People carve statues, showing the spirits or scenes from myths. Carved masks and shields are worn at dances, funerals and other ceremonies. They are often made of wood from the forest. The hornbill carving from Papua New Guinea (left) is a fertility symbol.

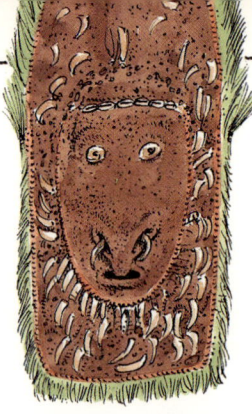

Ceremonial shield, Papua New Guinea

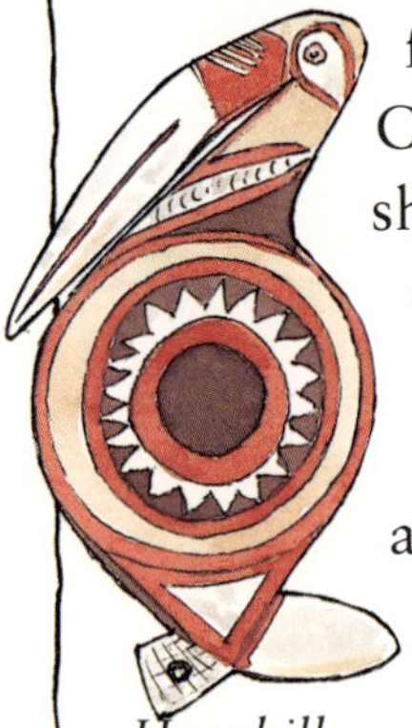

Hornbill carving for spirit house, Papua New Guinea

Roof disc from dancing house, South America

JEWELLERY

Jewellery is an important part of jungle costume. Amazon hunters wear jaguar tooth necklaces as symbols of strength.

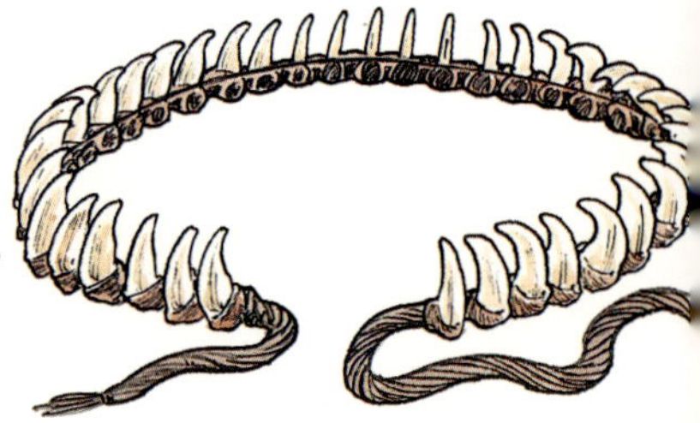

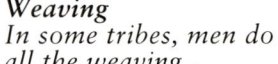

Jaguar tooth necklace, South America

The roof disc (left) is displayed in the houses of the Wayana people of South America. It shows animals from the three worlds - the sky, water and land.

Making pottery
Pots are made from clay mixed with ash.

Grater
All-important manioc graters are made from stone chips and board.

Decorating
This canoe paddle is painted with black soot and red seed juice.

Weaving
In some tribes, men do all the weaving.

24

COSTUME AND MAKE-UP

Among some tribes, a great deal of time and care is spent on getting ready for a dance (see next page) or another important ceremony. Only men are allowed to wear full ceremonial costume – it is believed to have magical powers. They paint their bodies with plant dyes. Different tribes wear different headdresses, made from toucan, parrot or bird of paradise feathers.

Each day, Wai Wai men paint on red make-up. Long, cane tubes cover their ponytails.

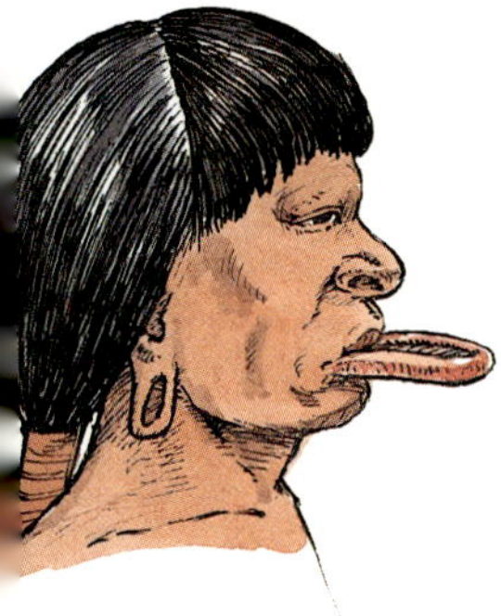

The Kayapo Indians stretch their lips.

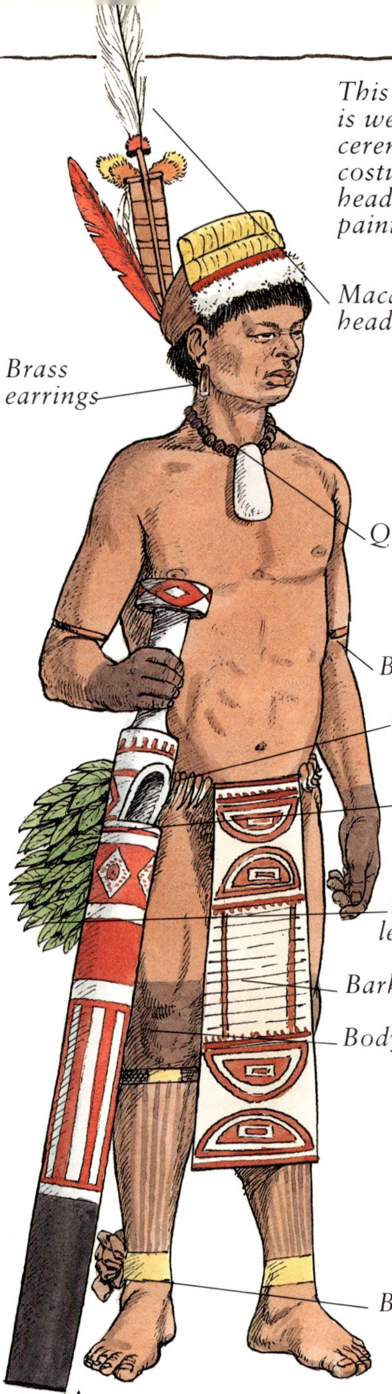

This Barasana hunter is wearing full ceremonial dancing costume, including headdress, body paint and jewellery.

- Macaw feather headdress
- Brass earrings
- Quartz necklace
- Bead arm bands
- Ocelot tooth belt
- Wooden dancing baton
- Sweet-smelling leaves
- Bark cloth apron
- Body paint
- Bark ankle band

SURVIVAL TIP 10

Don't be alarmed by people and dogs painted red! The Wai Wai of South America believe this protects them from evil spirits who can't see red.

Kamiura tribe   Amahuacan   Asmat tribe

MUSIC AND DANCING

Dances are held to celebrate many different occasions, such as initiation rites, funerals, maloca warming, honey gathering and so on. They are also the main form of entertainment and a chance to meet up with old friends. In South America, guests come from neighbouring malocas to join in the dancing and to drink manioc beer. The men wear full ceremonial costume, stamping their feet in time to the music. The women watch from the sidelines. The men sometimes take them by the hand to join in the dancing.

Panpipes

Flute

Whistle

Horn

Dancing
In some tribes, the dancing lasts all day and all night, starting early in the morning. The Wai Wai hold marathon dances, lasting three days and three nights.

MUSIC TO THE EARS

The dancers are accompanied by musicians playing instruments, such as panpipes made of reeds, bamboo flutes, horns and shellwhistles. They believe music summons the spirits.

A TRIAL OF STRENGTH

When a boy reaches adolescence, he has to undergo a series of initiation rites to prove his strength and courage. In the Barasana tribe, a boy has first to show off his hunting, tree-felling, canoeing and dancing skills. Then he is whipped by the shaman to test his courage and to make him braver.

Yage
Yage is a bitter liquid, made of bark mixed with water. The dancers drink it because it makes them hallucinate and see visions of the spirits.

CHEWING COCA

In many South American tribes, the men chew coca leaves during the dances and at other social occasions. The leaves contain drugs which help to keep you awake. Coca leaves are also toasted, crushed and mixed with ash to make a strong powder.

SURVIVAL TIP 11

Just as many Western adults do, rainforest people drink alcohol at ceremonies. They also take intoxicating drugs. They are used to these and know their effects. You do not – AVOID THEM!

GETTING ABOUT AND OUT

It's easy to lose your way, and your sense of direction, in the jungle. After a while, one tree looks very much like another. The thick vegetation hides any paths or tracks. You can't navigate by the sun or the stars, because it's very rarely that you can see them. Of course, rainforest people have many ingenious ways of finding their way through the jungle. Pay close attention to them! It's time to leave and you'll need their help.

WALK ON THE WILD SIDE

Hunters need to keep in touch with each other when they're stalking prey through the forest. But there's no point creeping along and firing silent arrows just to ruin it by shouting! So, they communicate by imitating animal and bird calls.

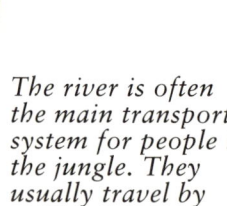

To indicate which way to go at a fork in the path, a hunter blocks one fork off with a bent sapling.

The river is often the main transport system for people in the jungle. They usually travel by canoe.

EXPLORER FACT

The famous explorer, David Livingstone (1813-1873), did most of his travelling by boat. It was much easier and quicker to paddle down a river than hack through the forest.

28

FLYING ANIMALS

Of course, if you were one of the animals shown here, you'd just fly, swing or glide your way through the forest. Bats and birds are the only real fliers, but some snakes, frogs and lizards can glide from branch to branch. So can the colugo, or flying lemur. It has wing-like flaps of skin between its wrists and ankles. Gibbons seem to fly because they swing so fast.

Flying snake

Gibbon

Colugo

Flying frog

Another way of marking a trail is to cut notches in the tree trunks. Then you won't go round in circles.

CANOE CARVING

Canoe-making needs a great deal of skill. Some people carve canoes out of whole tree trunks. They hollow out the inside, then heat it over a fire to open it up. Then they keep the sides apart by putting planks inside. These become seats. Other tribes make bark canoes.

SURVIVAL TIP 12

If you want to be rescued, you need to attract attention. Make a smoky fire with wet leaves – or get to a river, make a raft and float off in search of help.

RAINFOREST SURVIVAL

Rainforests are home to at least half of all the species of animals and plants in the world, as well as to people. In fact, one in five forms of life are only found in the Amazon rainforest. The jungles are treasure chests of medicines and other resources. Yet they are being destroyed so fast that by the year 2010 they may be gone.

RAINFORESTS AND THE WORLD

The rainforests play a crucial part in the climate. The trees take in carbon dioxide and release precious oxygen. When they are burned, they release carbon dioxide, adding to the greenhouse effect and global warming.

EXPLORER FACTS

People are still finding new ways of exploring the rainforests. In 1989, French scientists worked from this rubber 'raft' perched on the treetops of the jungle canopy.

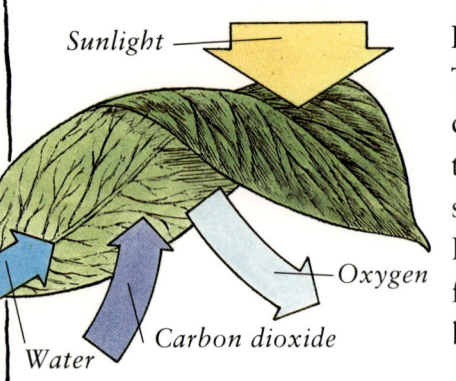

Sunlight
Oxygen
Water
Carbon dioxide

RAINFOREST PRODUCTS

The rainforests are being destroyed for their valuable timber and other resources, such as the rattan vine. Rattan is used to make furniture, mats and baskets.

SAVING THE RAINFORESTS

Many conservation groups are now involved in saving the rainforests and their people and wildlife. Why not join one of them to help?

GLOSSARY

Canopy The thick layer of tree branches and leaves over the rainforest.

Conservation The protection of wild animals, plants and wild places.

Epiphytes Plants such as orchids and bromeliads which grow on the branches of rainforest trees.

Greenhouse effect The build up of gases, such as carbon dioxide and methane, in the atmosphere. It traps the sun's heat and may be making the Earth too warm.

Humidity The amount of water vapour in the air. High humidity means that the air contains lots of water vapour. It makes it feel very sticky.

Jungle Strictly speaking, jungle is the thick, tangled mass of trees, shrubs and vines you see from the river bank or edge of a clearing. Also used simply to mean rainforest.

Malaria A fever-like disease, spread by mosquitoes. It can be fatal.

Maloca A type of communal house used by some South American tribespeople. To them, it represents the world itself.

Manioc A type of plant with potato-like tubers. It is the staple food of many South American tribespeople.

Nomads People who wander from place to place, in search of food for themselves or their animals. They never settle in one place for long.

Rainforest A hot, steamy forest which grows near the Equator. It is often described as jungle.

Shaman A tribe's medicine man.

Shrubs Plants with woody stems like trees, but much smaller than trees.

Strychnine A deadly poison.

Survival The ability to stay alive, even in difficult conditions.

Timber Trees that are cut down to provide wood for building, making furniture and so on.

Tuber A short, thick plant stem which grows underground.

INDEX

A
Amazon River, 6, 13
Arts and crafts, 24

B
Bates, Henry Walter, 17
Blow-pipes, 12, 13
Body painting, 25

C
Canoes, 16, 24, 28, 29
Canopy, 4, 30
Climate, 8, 9, 30
Clothes, 8, 10, 25, 26

D
Dancing, 24, 25, 26, 27
Dangerous animals, 18, 19
de Orellana, Francisco, 13
Drugs, 20, 27

E
Emergent layer, 5

F
Farming, 12, 17
Fawcett, Percy, 18
Fishing, 12, 16
Flying animals, 29
Food, 12-17
Frog, arrow-poison, 12, 18

G
Gardens, 17
Gathering food, 12, 14

H
Hammocks, 11

Hansen, Eric, 9
Homes, 10, 11, 17
Hunting, 12, 13, 18, 28

I
Initiation rites, 27

J
Jewellery, 24, 25
Jungle, 4
 definition of, 4

K
Kingsley, Mary, 15

L
La Condamine, 20
Language and
 communication, 22, 23, 28
Leeches, 9
Lip stretching, 25
Livingstone, David, 28

M
Make-up, 25
Maloca, 10, 11, 23, 26
Manioc, 14, 24, 26
Mosquitoes, 9, 18, 19
Music, 26
Myths, 22, 23, 24

N
Navigation, 28, 29

P
Plants, 20, 21
 dangerous, 20
 medicinal, 21

Poisons, 12, 16, 18, 19

R
Rainforest, 4, 5, 6, 7
 Amazon, 4, 5, 6, 8, 17, 30
 animals and plants, 5, 18, 19, 20, 21, 30, 31
 conservation, 30
 definition of, 4
 destruction of, 6, 7, 30
 layers of, 4, 5
 location of, 6, 7
 people of, 6, 7, 8
 resources, 15, 30
 types of, 5
Rubber, 20
Rubbish bird (pitohui), 19

S
Salt, 9
Schweizer, Albert, 23
Shelters, 10, 11
Shrub layer, 4
Snakes, 18, 19
Sweating, 8, 9

U
Understorey, 4

V
von Humboldt, Alexander, 19

W
Water, 21
Weapons, 12, 13, 16
Weather, 8, 9
Wickham, Henry, 20